Cat and Dog Play Hide and Seek

Written and illustrated by
Shoo Rayner

Collins

Where is Cat?

3

Is he under the table?

4

Is he behind the chair?

Is he under the bed?

Is he in the cupboard?

Where is Cat?

13

A story map

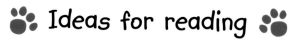 Ideas for reading

Written by Linda Pagett B.Ed (hons), M.Ed
Lecturer and Educational Consultant

Reading objectives:
- read and understand simple sentences
- read some common irregular words
- demonstrate understanding when talking with others about what they have read

Communication and language objectives:
- express themselves effectively, showing awareness of listeners' needs
- listen to stories, accurately anticipating key events and respond to what they hear with relevant comments, questions or actions
- develop their own narratives and explanations by connecting ideas or events
- give their attention to what others say and respond appropriately

Curriculum links: Personal, Social and Emotional Development

High frequency words: cat, and, dog, is, he, the, in

Interest words: where, under, table, behind, chair, bed, cupboard, oops

Word count: 27

Resources: small whiteboards, colour pens

Build a context for reading

- Look at the front cover together and introduce the characters Cat and Dog. (They can also be found in another Collins Big Cat book: *Cat and Dog, Lilac/Band 0.*)

- Ask the children to guess what is happening. *Are Cat and Dog playing a game? How is Cat trying to move? (He is creeping away.)*

- Read the title aloud and ask children if they have played hide and seek before. What are the rules?

- Look at the back cover, point out the blurb and explain what it is. Read the blurb together.

- Walk through the book and ask the children to say what is happening in the pictures. Discuss what the thought bubbles are saying.

Understand and apply reading strategies

- Ask the children to read aloud and at their own pace up to p13, pointing to each word as they read it.